tender machines

tender machines

J. MAE BARIZO

TUPELO PRESS

2023

Tender Machines
Copyright © 2023 J. Mae Barizo.

ISBN PB 978-1-946482-84-6
ISBN HC 978-1-946482-96-9

Library of Congress Cataloging-in-Publication Data
Identifiers: LCCN 2023003439
| ISBN 978-1-946482-84-6 (paperback) | 9781946482969 (hardcover)
Subjects: LCSH: Women--Poetry.
Classification: LCC PS3602.A77542 T46 2023 | DDC 811/.6--dc23/eng/20230228
LC record available at https://lccn.loc.gov/2023003439

Cover and text designed by adam bohannon.

First paperback edition May 2023

Tupelo Press
P.O. Box 1767
North Adams, Massachusetts 01247
(413) 664-9611 / Fax: (413) 664-9711
editor@tupelopress.org / www.tupelopress.org

Tupelo Press is an award-winning independent literary press that publishes fine fiction,
non-fiction, and poetry in books that are a joy to hold as well as read. Tupelo Press is
a registered 501(c)(3) non-profit organization, and we rely on public support to carry
out our mission of publishing extraordinary work that may be outside the realm of the
large commercial publishers. Financial donations are welcome and are tax deductible.

For my mother, my sister and my daughter.
And for my friend, L. M.

CONTENTS

"I don't see what women see in other women," I'd told Doctor Nolan in my interview that noon. "What does a woman see in a woman that she can't see in a man?"

Doctor Nolan paused. Then she said, "Tenderness."

SYLVIA PLATH

I.

the women

THE MOTHERS

We must be the inviolate
petals, always queering
towards the sun, must
be water on the lips of
flaming cities, quenching
the husbands, insatiable.
These days the abdomen
blossoms, but we must be
boneless, edible fish. We
must beg for bouquets
for absent sons. This is
how we know devotion:
listening to lovers sleep,
breathing like monster
trucks, wanting to soothe
them when the dream is
done. We march the sinking
avenues, finger the curls
at the baby's neck, hanging
from the brink at office
hour, gulping Xanax in
their white oblong shells.
Clouds can sleep but we
can never. Vigilant animals
on our hands and knees,
asking for it again and again.

SUNDAY WOMEN ON MALCOLM X BOULEVARD

My lungs grow black lilies
while I play Bach's *Ich ruf zu dir*

on the spinet in the Harlem room.
The light is getting longer

and the one love I keep hoarding
is still asleep while wildfires

bloom a few miles away. He too
must be locked in a room full

of music, waking slow. From
my window I can see inside

other chambers where my sisters
read the news of melting ice-caps

and the virus named after a crown;
other mothers and daughters tending

their small plunders. They wonder
how long to hold onto husbands, how

to skin a chicken, how to tend a fire
that burns thousands of miles away.

I breathe, alveoli burning, many-petaled
in the dark. As a child I used to stick

my finger into the flower's stamen
and lick, orange powder searing

my lips. See how my desire thrives?
Feeding on every living thing.

SURVIVAL SKILLS (SMALL ESSAY ON EXTINCTION)

Being able to dodge
a bullet, eat kale

with gusto, avoid
gluten altogether.

I couldn't decide
whether I should

stay or run faster—
how to be faithful?

Do genes play
a factor? Were

my ancestors
concubines or slaves?

The longer desire
takes to find an outlet

the less it can be contained.
Consider the fermata

in a sonata, practicing
always for disappearance.

FUGUE ON THE MAIDEN NAME OF MY MOTHER

There was a mad priest from Spain who impregnated women
in the village, among them my great-great-grandmother who
as the favored concubine was given the surname Miraflores
which translates to "Look at the flower!" Miraflores in legend
is high romance: "Miraflores, fountain-girded, where the trees
are many-birded. . . . Miraflores, name of beauty! May I earn
a lover's duty." In Don Quixote, Miraflores was an ancient
house, in its garden Oriana felt no further shadow should fall
upon her, raising hopes for my children's children, who will
have a different name dear colonizer, dear despoiler of my
ancestors, now that you are dead and almost forgotten with
your priest's habit and hungry cock and your dazzling Philippine
art collection and I am left here to procreate, to recreate
this history, my oppressor my settler my colonizer, my love.

WOMAN CONTEMPLATES HER COMPLICITY

I'm writing you in yoga clothes made in the country
my parents left behind, an archipelago of over seven
thousand islands. See the whites lounging in caftans
on catamarans, smiling and waving? They act kindly
when they hear my Oxford accent, if I'm wearing hair
product and Philippine pearls harvested from oysters
they slurp noisily. My grandmother is so poor she drinks
food supplements ("Ensure is cheaper than real food")
while we watch the whites stomp on the reefs. I marvel
at the succulence of buko and mangoes, not used to
these kinds of delights. I'm complicit, with my manicure
and expertly-dyed hair, watching the rich massaged by
natives on the beach. Whose side am I on? My skin, my
skin beneath the sun of my ancestors darkens so very easily.

WOMAN ON THE VERGE

If you've ever fallen asleep in your party dress
smoked out of a soft apple   darted your tongue

into a mouth because she told you she loved
Mozart piano concertos   ever cried in the Uber

or during the whale documentary   breastfed babies
on a public bus   ever paid a week's salary coloring

the grays   or cried into a hot tub full of younger
more pliable people   if you took the hormones

downloaded the meditation app   used the massage
chair as vibrator   stayed up till dawn watching

the sun rise over the Pacific   lying back and faking
it   because why not it's the Winter

of my fortieth year and best bleed when the blood
is hot   I tell you *I'm alive I'm alive*

PLEISTOCENE

It's just like she imagined: sporting
a blue backless gown, a radiologist
with cold hands, an X-ray room

that hasn't changed its look since 1969.
The doctor calls later, something cloudy
in the lungs. His voice makes her remember

losing the baby, little red leaf. And what if
she would have *wanted?* Scarlet lantern
moths, seasons later than usual, sweat slinking

on skin. What little deaths we leave
our children, our not-children. Tell her
the future will be soft, that the earth's not

getting hotter, that the lungs will heave
again before the stars burn out. Glacials
are so long, interglacials so short, the thunder

of mouths. She just wants to be the cold gleam
reaching back to the Pleistocene, hurtling.

ASTRONOISE

The child sleeps
and I find new ways
to write about stars.

Thinking of bandaged
light, scars on my arms
or the oldest bright

in the universe
moving through
astral storms

and drawing in ice
on earth's poles.
If the eye

is the corridor
to the spheres
I aimed to shape

a world where touch
didn't hurt because
it was so particular.

THE WOMEN

An evening of expected rain. Out the window clouds lifted
their skirts and the wind poured in. We were the mothers
lingering over the dessert tray, placing the sweets in our
mouths, one by one. We were the soothers and givers,
keepers of children and men. Those days, our skin bunched
up at the bra line, eyelids gathering like crinoline as it folds.
Yet standing there at the table, there was nothing in the world
we were in want of, not even the loves that had escaped us.
Whatever we suffered, we let go of willingly. To know we
were not the same women as before did not pain us. When
the others spoke their voices swept over us like bees hovering
over lilacs. Outside lights strobed over the Hudson; we watched
a white boat riding the crest of a wave, headed to sea. We
felt an ache we realized was happiness, almost unbearable.

small essays on disappearance

Morning in the city and the performance
that is Madison Avenue wearing diamond
studs for breakfast, my eyelashes crop
open and I rise believing in almost every
god, I didn't expect life to be kind to me
with my skin and second-hand pearls, at
school the other mothers' lips are bud-like;
melon-pink on top of immaculate incisors,
if I fixate on the other mothers I see them
as retrospectively luminous, what happens
to the past after it loses its radiance? All
my life sacrificed to the arrogance of cities,
their empires of skin.

Whittle of stilettos on the street, looming
towers gathering dollars as they rise, ring
tones vibrating and inaudible. The briefest-
glimpsed people are the most beautiful; when
the body is in pain it reorients itself, Death
takes us to third person but I don't think
I can stop writing about snow in the moment—

February and the sky was white
the streets were white and Barack
was paramount, what a fantastic
hour when she was born: keyholes
gushing, midwife thrusting needle
into skin, I remembered years ago
the quick slice of razors on wrists
what bliss, red aligning on the eaves
or beneath the skin. "May I eat
the candy necklace off my body?"
the child asks, miniature city of her
face, the more Time presses the more
beautiful they become—lover
husband mistress child—I played
Goldberg Variations as she slept
thinking of the geologic proportions
of Manhattan: *limestone, marble, malachite.*

White cool of milk, whine
of street machines, Schubert
steepling in my ear. The photo
of the child, backpack sagging
on her way to school, this static
moment my monocular vision
of love, nostalgia blooming
before the moment is even
done *click* an instant swirling
into disorder *click* this discrete
parcel of time *click* the photo
itself implying a world surging
beyond its edges—

The child's face is parallel
to mine, too small still
to know the performance
that is Madison Avenue
wearing tennis whites for
breakfast, men with pocket
squares and bleached front
teeth, white gold bangles
on thin wrists, my wrist
is small and scarred, I spy
stretch marks, curving
staircases and white marble
parquet. "What exactly does
bi-racial mean?" the child asks
black olive eyes peering up
at mine. That your father
is white your mother is not
and you have inherited a dark
church of brown hands.

Daughter, years ago
I watched the slowness
of people on sidewalks,
grief cascading like a
giant azalea then later
in the yellow bathroom
your father bandaging
the pink blooms of my
little wrists. I think of violins.
From my Manhattan bed
sirens yelp like pint-sized
dogs, the room is full of
noisy windows and every
so often I hear the Dominican
lady in the foyer singing
anywhere, anywhere—

It is just past eight thirty
in the city and I wanted
to write a poem about
currency but it turned out
to be about love, what I mean
is to live is to be rapacious:
thicket of string quartets,
the yellow cuts on my arm
that sting and sing the street
with its coffee-stained light.
This instant of sight binding
the world. Once, I loved
a woman, deciduous—

Before the towers fell
I loved for a time, carried
it around like a pacemaker
sing singing the concrete river I
loved I loved the red thunder
of her mouth the demolitions
blasting every block I ever
lived, clavicle and scapulae
clavier of spinal cord, I was
carnivore for love and yet
I could not have loved
it was only touch to keep
from disappearing.

I think of the veins
of arms, an exposure
of aspen leaves on skin
the children on the grass
their voices rising. To keep
myself present I memorize
their figures in the field
orientation of cheeks and
tiny feet, the day the towers fell
the sky was ultraviolet the light
blinded for an instant and then
fell into the sea, lace of branches
overhead masking the toxic
industry of dollars, daughter
the trees are infrared and without
fault tonight and every day I think
that we might die, I take you by
the hand and music pours down
the page, hear how the subway
trains slice through air? Pink
stripes on your socks, every
day you are so tall and I am
such a small mother.

tender archive

You blush like dawn and burn like a solar flame

HILDEGARD VON BINGEN

POSSIBILITIES OF EROS

The back of a woman's heel
flashes on concrete.

Later in the overgrowth
a garden. Touch: an arrow.

Hand undoes the fern.
Under foot, green
embroidery.

*

Voice that wings
itself to air.

What knits
two tongues? A bird
in the mouth

moves so gracefully.

*

Nearest you
the person wintered.

Caress unlocking
the veined leaf.

Lachrymose, Latin
for *like tears*.

*

Bodies dredged
from the river contained
trace chemicals, snow
on blue lips.

Kiss on the thigh, acid
rain snaking through air.

Room as hot sky, locked in.

*

Her arm, a glacier.

Before the earth falls
away *die Lichtung,* a clearing

in the green: everything
unconcealed.

SHADOW HAND

You clasped the hair
at my neck, pulling me
out of the ground.

Nape & blood
stitched up like
a witch wife.

My mouth saluted
you, monster—
shadow hand.

JETLAG

Morning scaled the window.
Pills stacked in the mouth: sandcastles.
Your finger, light saber.
Sickness needled the air.
Even the window went pale
Squinting at the gold teeth of the sun.

THE CAT

The cat is cackling about something.
Its white body bending over me.

Because the violins are silent
the night curves away without us noticing.

But the cat knows, tearing off feathers.

YELLOW SANS SERIF

I hold you in my fish memory
but can't return

Little fishes trading lips

Sleeves without arms
yellow sans serif

Little shirt that held
my hunger.

CLAVIER

She will be a string
plucked on the inside
of a piano.

Vibrating
between clavicles
an ocean sound.

It hurt to be
so pliant, twigs
beneath the fingers.

Hand covering mine
to keep the bird
from pulsing out.

[WE SWIM INTO GREEN DISASTERS]

We swim into
green disasters

Snow accumulating
beneath the tongue.

Eye to throat, a rash
appears. Imagine,

a flame furling
from the inside out.

*

The cats are quieting
down. I have told

no one about you.
Their eyes navigate

the beige ocean
of bed sheets watching

us wake, one by one.

*

Blue star
of smoke detector

to the green stars
of the feline eyes

sharpening then
blurred. I harbor you.

*

There is a cold
clock ticking
in my mouth.

In the bedroom
a puffin cries
into my pink
lace racerback.

In the night a noise
machine, in the morning
       a cantata.

*

I dreamt you
into bed but you
were cooking aubergines

in my childhood
home. Come
to bed, I said.

First we have
to clean the oven,
you answered.

*

And if you die, then
what. Lilacs in the rain

return me to childhood:
lapis lazuli, tiger's eye.

A lone swallow plummeting
        through peaks.

*

I wear your socks
after you have left.

Violet diagonal,
ribbed fabric, pink
worn heel.

The thread
stretches, then
disappears.

EXIT MUSIC

Tent of clothing, shadow veins.

Eye lash petals, a blue sock
unravels at the heel, pulling
fast as lids fall.

The spinet hums.

And you rise, remembering
to wind back the clocks.

II.

tender machines

TENDER MACHINES

Though he designed mechanical birds. Cloud
       ladders also, used to besiege city walls.
The hand then, which was Olympic in its grandeur,
       the shape of something identifiable
but not the same name as the river. She was
       like a crooked line of trees by the water
that kept usurping your personal space. Though
       that memory was out of focus still.
Though he fit inside her mind like an exquisitely
       gloved hand. A previous moment, susceptible
to being broken but which became ultimately more human
       in the process. Yes, she would rather have
this version of the film than relying on that memory.
       No, it was not her priori belief that any other
human could be so beautiful. That is why the path
       of the light took on a third world quality.
Yes, that is why she told him that when she was in love
       she was more susceptible to the killing cold.

*

LUX AETERNA

That morning again you hauled my arm to the window
and put a new dress on it. *Let me*, you said.
The street machines were singing and how young
we were and always eating. Buying food
at the bodegas, fleshy Jewish rolls, nectarines, skin-tight
plums. The way that day you held the phone
like a baby but it wouldn't stay still. Because the sky
was white, the streets were white and your hands
had me all over them. Because the light was blonde
the way we liked the boys then. Before
the curfews, before the sheltered dark. Tell me
that I remember it correctly, that the light
will lick and lick the damage clean. That it is not
ruin already. Tell me.

VIEW FROM AN APARTMENT

Scissored clouds with light snaking
through. Masks and jumpers, footsteps
like ants in a flurry. She craved bodegas
and foreign films. To walk out of a building
and squint, surprised by so many words.
There was wind outside, trees swaying
like uncertain eyelids. Sidewalks and sun
as it struck them. She knew that what
was written was meant to be forgotten.
Sometimes I sing so pretty it breaks my own heart.
She was humming into the hemisphere
but no one could hear it. Outside
the pedestrians gleamed like pinpricks.
Someone somewhere was walking away.

LOVE POEM IN THE SHAPE OF A COCHLEAR MECHANISM

The human ear a plastic thing.
When the boy returned to the city of angels
the ringing where the girl was told him
that America was ruthless and full

of silly coins. There was, inside
the memory, the rumor of a dollhouse;
all the furniture in immaculate order.
When the sound panel exploded a hand

was put forward once, then withdrawn.
The country splintering into a thousand
pieces. What an unruly thing an ear was.
Her voice as well, with its uncertain music.

MORNING IN A CITY

The dilemma always, is forgetting: the notion
that details cancel out the affect of a moment, beauty

concealed by particularities. Haydn sonatas played by
Pogorelich, for example, or the deep indigo of a certain

shirt. That the pianist's exaggerated bass notes and shifts
in tempi, the existence of such music in a room with

crooked walls is a departure from a world one cannot
give birth to, a room of undiluted sun. Or the sentiment

that overindulgence is a signal of tastelessness in Haydn
but not in Ravel. Because there is no one thing where

emotion corresponds in the same fashion as it does with
another. Just as there is no fixed reaction to this Adagio or

to the sound of the word *Dornauszieher* when it is whispered:
one who extracts thorns. I thought about this in the early morning

as the voice of my friend diminuendoed, sparse sentences
and all the while the underlying ostinato of desire. The sky

lightening to lavender and my memory faltering: Las Rocas,
mimosa tree, a cloud-hung sky. Longing because it is so full

of passing places. You are so forgettable my restless—your silly
mispronunciations, your hand slicing melon, that painting

that you love. Such tenderness, those sunrises with your hand at my
rib cage, our longing like a famine in a green country; my childhood

sonatas, limestone quarries I used to swim in where I caught crayfish
with my bare hands, the lilacs and their thousand petal tongues.

AT THE WHITNEY, THINKING ABOUT THE TREES

Impossible to ignore, the trees. You were alone
in a hospital bed, probably in an immodest gown.
Siri said—*distance is a vector quantity; distance is a primal
fact*—I was so afraid then of death that I kept silent,
eating continuously. At the museum there were no names
on the artwork; I kept taking pictures of clouds. Would
I love you more if you died? I wanted the future to be
uncertain because I was tired of being unsurprised. Did
you save the gif of me falling in the lake? You were silent
on social media. I googled 'I'm so mysterious I can't even
understand myself.' *Distance is displacement; distance is measured in*
In the museum, I wanted to touch everything on the walls.
Look, a bleeding cloud. A stranger was sewing up your incision.
On the screen the trees with their tender crimson scars.

UPON HEARING FUGUE NO. 23 FROM *WELL-TEMPERED CLAVIER,* BWV 893

"The naked thing is so tedious, that's why
I have such a love for tedium, I'm always

trying to transform the atonal to the tonal"
the letter said, after he couldn't answer

What is it you want? at Zabriskie Point. Our
bare legs submerged in a swarm of sand

mites, him pulling the socks on my feet,
me not knowing he'd be dead (cerebral

aneurysm) in a year's time. What's the word
for two people who've loved each other

without speaking for so long? The last time
I saw him I felt childhood approaching; fingers

on ivory, Bach ribboning through air. The fugue
with its mad counterpoint, my small & futile hands.

WALKING TO ZABRISKIE POINT, THINKING ABOUT THE SEA

There was tenderness
in the email: *I'm here
considering the obliteration*

of time zones. We who
had touched tentatively.
The birds were going

haywire in the sky—
mother hawk with a streak
of crimson on her chest—

focused on something
I could not see. Desire
was less the believing

what was hidden and more
like being shipless (for the first
time being seen.) My whole life—

pity!—I'd been dormant. Thorns
nicked my leg; the idea of us
hurtling. What if our paths

were asymptotic, as the birds?
Pity in our previous lives
we'd never seen the desert,

sunlight thrashing the canyon, skin.
I wanted you to view my body
as ineffable, an ocean—

WOMAN WAKES IN ANOTHER TIME ZONE

I wake up too close
to the underside of your arm—

a flaccid white fish
against my brown cheek.

My eyes are still closed
but I've memorized

your body, I don't have to look
to see you aged and aimless,

landscape of non-cancerous
but severely atypical moles

on the skin. I put my hand
in yours, and when you wake

with your opulent anxiety, reaching
for your pills and phone, scrolling

maniacally, I see that you've
refused the one thing

I'm offering. At midnight
I lie upstairs while you

are at the piano, a staircase
away from me. To be

near you is not ordinary, a flame
at its center, furling

from the inside out, heart
flailing. Still, how many

dawns you've lain absent,
my solitary mornings

on the terrace, missing
you, a staircase away.

I've watched the palm trees
a hundred times now, the way

they stand in solidarity,
constant and separate, against

the blue. Even as I hear
you playing Bowie

through the floorboards
I think maybe this

is not what I made it out
to be. Soon

you'll be cranky from hunger
and we'll scramble

eggs together, sit on
the porch, share

a single cigarette. *Here,*
I'll say. *I'm here.* Will you pretend

I haven't spoken? Maybe it's not
you I long for, but the woman

I once was, in another
time zone, looking at the trees.

THE MOUNTAIN

We were sitting shoulder to shoulder looking at the fires
in the canyon and I said something about distance, desire

moving from archive to digital, I was thinking of starting
something, despite time zones or children, husbands

or wives. The sky parted an instant, I thought I saw
cloud shadows cross your face but it was only trees

cleaving, map-work, the paths of our ancestors—
Auschwitz, Manila, Manhattan—lit up in the night. Blue

star of smoke detector, green of the cat's eyes. Us
talking and not touching until dawn, when we could

no longer see the fires but smelled them: brushwood,
synthetic polymers, skin. I closed my eyes. Then

I stood up and called an Uber, taking your face in my
hands, unsure still of what anchored us to the mountain.

ANDANTE CANTABILE

All morning with fingers on the strings
Beethoven on repeat
A photo of my grandmother
Clicked a thousand times
The past stalks with its slaking fire
It is the autumn of my fortieth year
My follicles are turning dry
See the muteness of my hands?
A love I once gave away
Haunts me everywhere.

NEW YORK, NOVEMBER

Today, my restless, yellow leaves
are thrashing through the wind.
The air in this city is thick
with fear and want and every
day the men and women
start to build again. Our lives
as we keep track of them
are acted out in simple
gestures: hand to mouth,
a gasp, clear-cut kiss
or not. Nothing harmful
nothing said. The things
we never speak of are like
the lost debris or yellow leaves
in any city, any fall. But
something tells us this
is different. Maybe it's
that sad, burnt scent
without a name. Perhaps
it's just New York, miles
from where you are.
All I can really be sure
of these days are the words
I write you from my crowded
heart, and the yellow leaves
and the way one season
meets the next, violently.

CODA

And what is it you hate? she asked.
Bureaucracy. And what is it you love?
he asked. *Rivers.* They walked and walked
until all the colors faltered. They drank
until even the grass felt ill. So many
days so few words and when it was dawn
nothing but birds flew out of their mouths.

ACKNOWLEDGEMENTS

The author gratefully acknowledges the following publications where these poems, or versions thereof, first appeared or are forthcoming:

Poetry, "The Mothers," and "The Women"

Bennington Review, "Fugue on the Maiden Name of My Mother," (formerly titled "Woman Considers the Plights of her Ancestors")

At Length, "Small Essays on Disappearance"

Bellingham Review, "Lux Aeterna"

Denver Review, "Love Poem in the Shape of a Cochlear Mechanism"

Iowa Review, "Tender Machines," (formerly titled "Love Poem from a Replicant")

Bellevue Review, "At the Whitney, Thinking about the Trees"

Ploughshares, "The Mountain"

Antietam Review: "New York, November"

Spoon River Poetry Review: "Morning in a City"

Tishman Review: "Walking to Zabriskie Point, Thinking About the Sea"

Four Quartets: Poetry in the Pandemic (Tupelo Press): "The Mothers;" "Lux Aeterna;" "New York, November;" "View from an Apartment;" "Sunday Women on Malcolm X Boulevard;" "Survival Skills: Small Essay on Extinction;" "At the Whitney, Thinking about the Trees"

Thank you to Kristina Marie Darling, Jeffrey Levine and everyone at Tupelo Press. Grateful for Richard Scheiwe, Timothy Liu, Askold Melnyczuk, Major Jackson, Phillip Lopate, Amy Gerstler, Ed Ochester, Katie Pawluk, Kyle Dacuyan and Cathy Lin Che, who saw these poems in their early forms. Thank you to Leslie

Maslow, Jill Horwitz, Maxwell Neely-Cohen, Vikram Rajan, Wolfram and Ada Koessel, and my father, Daniel Barizo. Thank you to my fellow mothers: Ophelia Barizo, Amanda Barizo, Elizabeth Lanning, Ligaya Mishan, Sarah Gambito, Maya Pindyck, Sarah Ruhl, Megan Galbraith, Asha Babat, Katie Schuele, Tamar Ettun, Rio Cortez and Wendy S. Walters. To my family, friends, students and teachers: thank you.

NOTES

"Morning in a City" is after Robert Hass.
"Woman on the Verge" is after Kim Addonizio.

ABOUT THE AUTHOR

CAROL GIMBEL

Born in Toronto to Filipino immigrants, J. Mae Barizo is a poet, essayist and multidisciplinary artist who works at the intersection of poetics, media and performance. Her work has been anthologized in books published by W.W. Norton, Atelier Editions and Harvard University Press. She is the recipient of fellowships and awards from Bennington College, Mellon Foundation, Critical Minded, Jerome Foundation and Poets House. An advocate of cross-disciplinary work, she has collaborated with artists such as Salman Rushdie, Mark Morris and the American String Quartet. She is on the faculty of The New School and lives in New York City.

CPSIA information can be obtained
at www.ICGtesting.com
Printed in the USA
JSHW080904120623
42984JS00004B/14